On your baptism

Presented to:

Michael

From:

Loren and Judy Krase

Date:

April 12, 2009

HAPPY EASTER!

HONOR
B O O K S

07 06 05 04 03   10 9 8 7 6 5 4 3 2 1

Happy Easter!

ISBN 1-56292-089-8
Copyright © 2003 Honor Books,
An Imprint of Cook Communications Ministries
P.O. Box 55388
Tulsa, Oklahoma 74155

Compiled by Lisa Hughes

Introduction

Easter is much more than just a day—it's a season that celebrates life, hope, and new beginnings. The Easter season tells a story—the story of the Savior's death, His glorious resurrection, and our hope for transformed lives.

Feel the excitement of the Easter season as you turn the pages of this book. The quotes, scriptures, poetry, and traditions will inspire you, touch your heart, and make you smile. We have included a read-along story for children at the end for your family to share.

Happy Easter!

*M*ay Easter Day

To thy heart say,

"Christ died and rose for thee."

May Easter night

On thy heart write,

"O Christ, I live to Thee."

Easter Tradition

The custom of wearing new clothes on Easter Sunday can be traced back to A.D. 300 when Constantine, the first Christian emperor, decreed that the members of his court should wear their finest clothes on Easter as a sign of the importance of the occasion.

Rise, for Christ the Lord arose,
Victor over all His foes;
Rise, with all the souls of men,
Into light and life again;
"Rise, flowers, rise!"

Ye happy bells of Easter Day!
Ring! Ring! Your joy
Thro' earth and sky;
Ye ring a glorious word.
The notes that swell in gladness tell
The rising of the Lord!

Easter Activities

To create your own little Easter chick, hard-boil an egg and dye it yellow. Using yellow construction paper, cut out the shapes of a beak, tail, pair of wings, and two webbed feet. Glue the parts onto the egg; then use a black marker to draw in the two eyes.

Did You Know?

The Dutch brought the traditions of the Easter egg and the Easter rabbit to America when they settled in Pennsylvania in the 1700s. The Dutch children used hats, bonnets, or fancy paper to prepare nests for the "Oschter Haws" or Easter Rabbit. Over the years the hats were replaced by elaborate Easter baskets. The children believed that if they had been good, the Easter Rabbit would come on Easter Eve and lay colorful eggs in their nests.

Welcome, happy morning! Age to age shall say:

Hell today is vanquished; Heaven is won today.

Lo! the Dead is living, God for evermore;

Him their true Creator, all his works adore.

O death, where is thy sting?
O grave, where is thy victory?

1 Corinthians 15:55 KJV

Easter says you can
put truth in a grave,
but it won't stay there.

Waken, sleeping butterflies,
Burst your narrow prison;
Spread your golden wings and rise,
For the Lord is risen;
Spread your wings and tell the story,
How He rose, the Lord of glory.

Did You Know?

On March 27, 1513, the Spanish explorer Juan Ponce de Léon discovered the peninsula of Florida while he searchd for the legendary Fountain of Youth. He named the land Florida because he made his discovery on Easter Sunday, and the Easter season was called *Pascua Florida* (Flowery Easter) in native Spain.

Did You Know?

A Dutch navigator named Jakob Roggeven discovered an island in the South Pacific on Easter Sunday, 1722; he named it Easter Island. It is approximately 2,200 miles off the western coast of Chile, and numerous stone carvings made from soft volcanic stone are located there. These statues of gigantic heads are ten to forty feet high and weigh up to fifty tons.

Death hath no more dominion over him.

Romans 6:9 KJV

*T*omb, thou shalt not hold Him longer;
Death is strong, but Life is stronger;
Stronger than the dark, the light;
Stronger than the wrong, the right;
Faith and Hope triumphant say
Christ will rise on Easter Day.

Did You Know?

In the 1880s, Mrs. Thomas P. Sargent of Philadelphia discovered the white trumpet lilies in Bermuda. She brought the bulbs back to the United States; and this Bermuda lily soon became known as the Easter lily— the favored flower for decoration at Easter time.

Easter Activities

To create an Easter flower bouquet, place a glass upside-down on a piece of colored tissue paper, draw around the rim, and cut out the circles. Stack three circles on top of each other—flower petals. Shape the petals by cutting curves around the edges. Insert a pin in the middle of the three petals. Hold the pin against a piece of thick craft wire—flower stem. Use different colored tissue paper, different size cups, and different designs to create a variety of flowers.

Did You Know?

The Easter basket did not become popular until the late 1800's, when candy became more common, thanks to a growing number of small candy manufacturers.

Did You Know?

In 1933, Paul H. King originated the idea of selling Easter seals as a fund-raising device for the International Society for Crippled Children. He believed the rehabilitation of crippled children that led to fuller lives and more activities for them harmonized with the meaning of Easter—Resurrection and New Life.

Snowdrop, lift your timid head,
All the earth is waking,
Field and forest, brown and dead,
Into life are breaking;
Snowdrops, rise and tell the story
How He rose, the Lord of glory.

Lilies! lilies! Easter calls,
Rise to meet the dawning
Of the blessed light that falls
Thro' the Easter morning;
Ring your bells and tell the story,
How He rose, the Lord of glory.

Did You Know?

The Easter bonnet began as a wreath of flowers or leaves, with the circle symbolizing the roundness of the sun.

The great Easter truth is not that we are to live newly after death, but that we are to be new here and now by the power of the resurrection.

Jesus said to her,
"I am the resurrection and the life.
He who believes in me
will live, even though he dies;
and whoever lives and
believes in me will never die."

John 11:25–26

Easter Activities

To make hollow eggs, use eggs that have been kept at room temperature for several hours. Shake the eggs to break up the yolks. Using a needle, make a hole in the bigger end and move the needle back and forth to make the hole a little larger. Use the same needle to make a smaller hole in the small end of the egg. Place your lips over the second hole and blow the egg out through the larger hole and into a bowl. Clean the shell and stand it up to dry. Use the egg yolk and whites to make omelets or cakes. Color and decorate your hollow eggs with paint, markers, feathers, sequins, and beads.

Did You Know?

The "look-inside" Easter egg originated either in Lithuania or Latvia. It is completely edible because it is made of fondant—a sweet, creamy sugar paste. The egg has a round opening at one end. When you look inside the opening, you see a sculptured landscape made of fondant that usually includes hills, trees, bushes, houses, chickens, rabbits, and tiny eggs. The outside of the egg is decorated with flowers and lacy edges.

H A P P Y   E A S T E R !

Easter Bunny Cupcakes

One cupcake mix
White frosting
Shredded coconut

Large marshmallows
Cloves

Use your favorite cupcake recipe. Once baked, invert the cupcakes onto a platter.
Spread white frosting on them; then sprinkle with shredded coconut. Use a large
marshmallow to create the head and a half of a marshmallow for the tail. Use
pieces of a large marshmallow and shape them into the two ears. Insert whole
cloves or halves of black jellybeans for the eyes, one red hot for the mouth, and
strands of coconut for the whiskers.

Easter Ice-cream Bunny

To make an ice-cream bunny, use firm vanilla ice cream and make a large scoop for the body of the bunny and a smaller scoop for the head. Set the two scoops on top of each other. Place about five miniature marshmallows on a toothpick. Make two of these and place them on the smaller scoop of ice cream to create the rabbit's ears. Decorate with red hots or jellybeans for the eyes and marshmallows for the mouth and tail. Place in the freezer until ready to serve.

*I*n the bonds of death He lay
Who for our offence was slain;
But the Lord is risen to-day,
Wherefore let us all rejoice.
Singing loud, with cheerful voice,
Hallelujah!

Easter Activities

To create simple Easter Place Cards, begin by folding white cardstock paper in half. Use markers to draw grass on the bottom of one side of the card. Above the grass, write the guest's name. Around the name draw and color Easter rabbits. Glue cotton balls in place for the bunny tails.

If Easter means anything to modern man
it means that eternal truth is eternal.
You may nail it to the tree, wrap it up
in grave clothes, and seal it in a tomb;
but "truth crushed to earth, shall rise again."

[Jesus] then began to teach them that the Son of Man must suffer many things and be rejected by the elders, chief priests and teachers of the law, and that he must be killed and after three days rise again.

Mark 8:31

A kiss at Christmas and
an egg at Easter

*E*aster says to us that despite everything to the contrary, his will for us will prevail, love will prevail over hate, justice over injustice and oppression, peace over exploitation and bitterness.

Did You Know?

The custom of coloring eggs at Easter seems to be a very old one. In 1290, King Edward I of England purchased 450 eggs that were to be colored or covered with leaf gold and given to the Royal Household.

Did You Know?

Originally, onionskins boiled in water were used to color eggs a light yellow. Then the eggs were boiled with flowers, logwood chips, or leaves to create other colors. Spinach leaves or anemone petals were used to create green, logwood chips for purple, gorse blossom or hickory bark for yellow, cochineal or madder root for red, and coffee or walnut shells for brown. An egg dyed red traditionally symbolized the blood of Christ. Today, vegetable dyes are used to create many brilliant colors.

The best news the
world ever had came
from a graveyard.

"He is not here, but is risen."

Luke 24:6 KJV

"Christ the Lord is risen today,"
Sons of men and angels say.
Raise your joys and triumphs high;
Sing, ye heavens, and earth reply.

Lift your voices in
triumph on high,
For Jesus is risen and
man cannot die.

The God of our fathers raised Jesus from the dead—
whom you had killed by hanging him on a tree.
God exalted him to his own right hand as Prince
and Savior that he might give repentance
and forgiveness of sins to Israel.

Acts 5:30-31

Easter Traditions

The Pennsylvania Dutch were well known for an Easter decoration called the Easter egg bird. This was a decorated eggshell in which four holes were made to insert a handcrafted head, wings, and tail of a bird. Another opening was made on the shell so that the bird could be attached to a piece of thread and displayed in the home.

Easter Traditions

In Pennsylvania in the nineteenth century, it was customary for men and children to engage in egg-eating contests. On Easter Sunday and Monday they also played a game called "picking eggs" that was designed to test the strength of eggshells by hitting the ends of eggs together. The broken egg was awarded as a prize to the person whose egg remained whole.

*O*ur Lord has written the promise of
resurrection, not in books alone,
but in every leaf in springtime.

*E*aster is a day to fan the ashes of dead hope, a day to banish doubts and seek the slopes where the sun is rising, to revel in the faith which transports us out of ourselves and the dead past into the vast and inviting unknown.

Did You Know?

One legend states that Simon of Cyrene, who carried
Christ's cross for Him, was actually an egg-peddler.
When he returned to his basket of eggs after his
somber walk with the Cross, he found all the eggs in
his basket beautifully decorated.

Easter in Other Countries

The people of Mexico create cascarones for Easter. These are blown out eggs filled with confetti and then the holes are sealed with brightly colored tissue paper "hats." They are then cracked on people's heads. Some people say that the cracked egg symbolizes Christ breaking out of His tomb.

Come, ye saint, look here and wonder,
See the place where Jesus Lay;
He has burst His bands asunder;
He has borne our sins away;
Joyful tidings.
Yes, the Lord has risen to-day.

This Jesus God raised up, and of that all of us are witnesses.

Acts 2:32 NRSV

Did You Know?

The first White House Easter Egg Roll was held on Easter Monday in 1878. President Rutherford B. Hayes and First Lady Lucy Hayes hosted the event, which took place on the South Lawn.

Easter Traditions

Egg rolling was another popular sport that is still
practiced today in some parts of the world. People roll
colored, hard-boiled eggs down a hill to see whose
egg can remain unbroken for as long as possible.

55

'Twas a thief that said the
last kind word to Christ:
Christ took the kindness
and forgave the theft.

[The criminal said,] "We are punished justly, for we are getting what our deeds deserve. But this man has done nothing wrong." Then he said, "Jesus, remember me when you come into your kingdom." Jesus answered him, "I tell you the truth, today you will be with me in paradise."

Luke 23:41-43

Easter Traditions

Following World War II, an annual Easter Egg Rolling Contest was held in New York's Central Park. Children, age five to twelve, used wooden spoons to roll wooden eggs along an established lane. The winners received toys and other gifts.

Easter Activities

The German Egg Blowing Game is played by placing a blown egg in the center of a table, where guests have been seated. One person blows the egg across the table to the other side. The person who is closest to the egg responds by blowing it back. No one is allowed to touch the egg, and anyone who lets the egg fall off the table is automatically out of the game. The last person at the table is the winner.

O chime of sweet Saint Charity,
Peal soon that Easter morn
When Christ for all shall risen be,
And in all hearts new-born!

"I, when I am lifted up from the earth,
will draw all men to myself."

John 12:32

Did You Know?

South Africa is the home for the largest Easter Egg
ever made. The egg was made entirely of
marshmallow and chocolate. It weighed 4,068 kilos
and was 7.65 meters high.

Did You Know?

On March 20, 1999, the world's largest Easter-egg hunt was held in Victoria, Australia, as a means to raise funds for the Vision Australia Foundation. Army troops hid about 150,000 chocolate Easter eggs that were provided by Cadbury's. Approximately 3,000 children participated in this event that was coordinated by companies all over Australia.

They took palm branches and
went out to meet him, shouting,
"Hosanna!"
"Blessed is he who comes in the name of the Lord!"
"Blessed is the King of Israel!"

John 12:13

He will swallow up death in victory;
and the Lord GOD will wipe away
tears from off all faces.

Isaiah 25:8 KJV

Did You Know?

The most ornate Easter eggs are actually not eggs at all. Rather, they are called Fabergé eggs and were created over one hundred years ago by a jeweler named Carl Fabergé in Russia. He handcrafted these elaborate eggs out of gold, silver, and jewels. When opened, each egg usually displays a hidden treasure, such as tiny figures of people, animals, or buildings. At Easter time, the Russian tsar would give these exquisite eggs to his friends and family.

Lenten Season

Shrovetide

Shrovetide or *Carnival* is the name for the last three or four days before Ash Wednesday and the beginning of Lent. All the days in Shrovetide have special names and customs associated with them, including Egg Saturday, Quinquagesima Sunday, Collop Monday, and Shrove Tuesday.

Egg Saturday

The Saturday before Ash Wednesday was once called Egg Saturday because children traveled to various houses and begged for eggs. The eggs they received were to be eaten before the beginning of Lent. If they were not given any eggs at a particular home, they threw broken dishes at the front door.

Collop Monday

The Monday of Shrovetide was once called Collop Monday. *Collop* is an old English word that means a cut of cured meat. All bacon, eggs, and fried collops of meat were supposed to be consumed by Collop Monday so that none would be left when Lent began.

Shrove Tuesday

In England as well as other countries, the day before Ash Wednesday is still known as Shrove Tuesday, Pancake Tuesday, Guttit Tuesday, or Goodish Day—due to the number of good things eaten then. It was customary to make pancakes on this day because the cooking fat, butter, and eggs used in the preparation had to be consumed prior to the beginning of Lent.

Shrovetide Pancakes

2 cups all-purpose flour
Dash of salt

2 beaten eggs
Milk

Mix together the flour, salt, beaten eggs, and just enough milk to make the batter thin. Grease a frying pan or pancake griddle and get it very hot. Pour three to four tablespoons of the batter onto your pan or griddle. Bake until golden brown on one side then flip over to the other side.

Did You Know?

After the Reformation, the church bell that had once been used to call Christians to confession during Shrovetide became known as the Pancake Bell—the signal for pancakes to be me made and for the sports, games, and other festivities to begin.

Fat Tuesday

In Sweden, Shrove Tuesday is known as Fat Tuesday. On this day the people eat *semlas,* or Fat Tuesday buns, which are big buns made out of wheat flour and filled with almond paste and whipped cream. The buns are served in bowls of hot milk. In Iceland, these *semlas* are called "cream buns," and Fat Tuesday is called Bursting Day because everyone eats an excessive amount of food.

Lent Traditions

In various parts of England, egg shackling, a popular game played on Shrove Tuesday. To play this game, children write their names on eggs and bring them to school. The eggs are then placed in a sieve and shaken until only one is left whole. The child whose egg is unbroken receives a cash prize, and the cracked eggs are either sent to a local hospital or returned home to make pancakes.

Lent Traditions

In 1950, housewives in Liberal, Kansas, U.S.A., challenged the housewives of Olney, Buckinghamshire, England, to a pancake race on Shrove Tuesday. The British housewives readily accepted the challenge, and since then, the International Pancake Day Race has become an annual event. Courses of identical distance are set up in each location, and the times of each of the winners are compared by telephone.

Ash Wednesday

The first day of Lent was formerly referred to as the "Beginning of the Fast." However, in A.D. 1099, Pope Urban II introduced the name *Ash Wednesday*. On this day, many Christians participated in a ceremony where blessed ashes were placed on their foreheads in the form of a cross. Then, a priest said, "Remember, man, that thou art dust, and to dust thou shalt return."

Did You Know?

Many years ago, most Christians did not eat meat, cheese, butter, cooking fats, or eggs during Lent—a period of forty days. In present day, Christians often give up something they enjoy, like candy or ice cream. In addition to being a period of fasting, Lent was also designed to be a time of mourning. People were expected to give up various entertainments and festivities. The atmosphere at the church reflected this state of mourning: there were no floral decorations or organ music. In many countries the women dressed in black and wore no jewelry.

Lent Traditions

To help count down the days of Lent, many Greeks cut out a paper figure of a nun. She did not have a mouth, since fasting was a crucial part of Lent; her hands were crossed in prayer; and she had seven feet, one for each of the seven weeks of Lent. One of the feet was torn off at the end of each week. Another method used in Greece was sticking seven feathers into an onion or a potato. This was hung from the ceiling and used in a similar fashion.

Lent Traditions

In the United States and Great Britain, hot cross buns are a popular food during Easter. These sweet rolls are stuffed with raisins and candied fruit; then sugar frosting is used to form a cross on the top of the buns. Initially, these hot cross buns were baked and eaten only on Good Friday, but now they are baked all through the period of Lent.

Fourth Sunday of Lent

In Luxembourg, the fourth Sunday of Lent is called *Bretzelsonndeg*,
which means Pretzel Sunday. On this day the boys present to their
girlfriends decorated cakes that look like pretzels. If the girl
admires her suitor, she responds on Easter Sunday by offering him
a hollow decorated egg filled with bonbons and by walking with
him to the park. On leap year, the tradition is reversed: the girl
gives the pretzel cake and the boy gives the Easter egg.

Fourth Sunday of Lent

The fourth Sunday in Lent is called Mid-Lent Sunday or Mothering Sunday in England. Children return to their mothers' homes to visit them and bring them flowers, simnel cakes, and other gifts to celebrate this day.

Did You Know?

Mothering Sunday never became an established custom in the United States. However, in 1907, Anna Jarvis, of Philadelphia, decided that there should be one day in the year when children honored their mothers. She organized a special service to be held in a local church, and she asked the attendees to wear white carnations. The service was a huge success. In 1914, largely due to her efforts, Congress determined the second Sunday in May to be Mother's Day.

Easter Traditions

It was customary for young men to send gloves to their girlfriends on *Easter Eve.* If the girlfriend accepted the gloves and wore them to church on Easter Sunday, it meant the courtship was progressing very well and would probably result in marriage.

Easter Traditions

In Russia on Easter weekend, young women are given Easter charms shaped like eggs. The eggs are usually made of semiprecious stones, like quartz and jade. The charms are placed on a necklace, and a girl's popularity is judged by the number of charms she receives.

God forbid that I should
glory, save in the cross of
our Lord Jesus Christ.

Galatians 6:14 KJV

*T*each me, my God, to bear my cross
As Thine was borne;
Teach me to make of every loss
A crown of thorn.

Thou art the Sun of other days,
They shine by giving back thy rays.

Spring bursts today,
For Christ is risen and
all the earth's at play.

Every noble crown is, and
on earth will forever be,
a crown of thorns.

"Easter"

The air is like a butterfly
With frail blue wings.
The happy earth looks at the sky
And sings.

Easter in Other Countries

In Switzerland tiny flowers, leaves, and other decorations are attached to the eggs prior to boiling them in an onion peel. This technique results in an elaborate white pattern on a tinted background. Sometimes a design or message is traced on an already dyed egg with a white wax pencil; other times a knife is used to scratch off some of the dye and to create an elaborate white design.

Easter in Other Countries

The Easter eggs in Hungary are generally white and decorated with a red flower pattern. The pattern is first traced on with wax; then the eggs are covered with cold paint. They usually contain a message, scripture verse, or picture of a man and woman in costume. The children exchange their eggs with one another as expressions of friendship. In some parts of the country the eggs are hung on little Easter trees that young men place outside the homes of the girls they wish to court.

Come, ye saints, look here and wonder,
See the place where Jesus lay;
He has burst His bands asunder;
He has borne our sins away;
Joyful tidings,
Yes, the Lord has risen today.

If you confess with your mouth,
"Jesus is Lord," and believe in
your heart that God raised him
from the dead, you will be saved.

Romans 10:9

Easter Traditions

The people in Poland and the Ukraine call their Easter eggs *pysanki*, which means "written eggs." A needle or small metal tube is used to draw designs or pictures on the eggs with wax. The designs are often geometrical or abstract patterns, and Christian symbols like the fish and the cross are also often used. Once the design is completed, the eggs are then dyed, and the wax is melted off. It often takes a person several days to create just one of these elaborate eggs.

Easter Traditions

Years ago, Polish girls presented their suitors with thirty to one hundred *pysanki* eggs that they had either decorated themselves or hired someone else to do. The decorated eggs were wrapped up in a handkerchief embroidered with the young suitor's initials along with other small presents like flowers, nuts, or tobacco. The young man was expected to reciprocate by giving the girl a piece of dress material, colorful ribbons, or a kerchief.

*A*ll Christian worship is a witness of
the resurrection of Him who liveth
for ever and ever. Because He lives,
"now abideth faith, hope, charity."

Awake, thou wintry earth—
Fling off thy sadness!
Fair vernal flowers, laugh forth
Your ancient gladness!
Christ is risen.

Easter Traditions

Egg shackling was a popular game played at Easter time in England and many European countries. Boys held hard-boiled eggs in their right hands and attempted to smash as many other eggs as possible while keeping their own eggs whole.

Easter Traditions

The Pennsylvania Dutch introduced the tradition of an Easter egg tree. They used needles to poke holes in eggs; then they blew the contents out. The eggshells were painted and decorated, and loops of colorful ribbon were pasted on the eggs so that they could be placed tip downwards on an evergreen or leafless tree. The Easter tree was then placed on a table in the center of the room. It was decorated, not only with the painted eggs, but also with ornaments, sugar people, cake animals, pieces of chocolate, and candy. Underneath the tree, an Easter rabbit or lamb was placed on the table to watch over all of the gifts.

Christ has turned all our
sunsets into dawns.

Ride on, ride on in majesty!
In lowly pomp ride on to die:
Bow thy meek head to mortal pain:
Then take, O God, thy power and reign.

Easter in Other Countries

In Scotland and northern England, a custom called "lifting" or "heaving" was popular on Easter Monday. A "chair" was made out of people's hands, and a person was tossed into the air three times and then kissed. The men "lifted" the women on Easter Monday, and the women "lifted" the men on Easter Tuesday. This custom was intended to represent Christ's resurrection.

Easter in Other Countries

In Popayán, Colombia, on the Tuesday before Easter, a ceremony called the Feast of the Prisoners takes place. The archbishop, various government officials, and other people form a procession to the prison, bringing with them an abundance of food. The prisoners are served as they listen to speeches. In a gesture representing the choosing of Barabbas, one of the prisoners is selected, presented with donations of food and money, and released from the prison.

In vain with stone the cave they barred;
In vain the watch kept ward and guard;
Majestic from the spoiled tomb.
In pomp of triumph Christ is come.

They found the stone rolled away
from the tomb, but when they
entered, they did not find
the body of the Lord Jesus.

Luke 24:2-3

The stone at the tomb
of Jesus was a pebble to
the Rock of Ages inside.

Angels, roll the rock away;
Death, yield up thy mighty prey:
See, He rises from the tomb,
Glowing with immortal bloom.
Al-le-lu-ia! Al-le-lu-ia!
Christ the Lord is risen today!

Easter in Other Countries

During Holy Week in Champagne, France, it has been the custom since the thirteenth century to hold a jousting tournament. Before the jousting begins, the young men ride their horses through the town, carrying long lances. They also carry a large wooden sculpture of Jesus, which they place on a platform in front of the church

"*Easter Week*"

Palm Sunday

Did You Know?

The majority of the palms used on Palm Sunday in the United States is harvested in Florida, whose state tree happens to be the cabbage palm. Thousands of acres of cattle land in this state are leased for the sole purpose of cutting the cabbage palm to use in church services on Palm Sunday.

Did You Know?

On the Saturday evening before Palm Sunday in Yugoslavia, it is customary for a young girl to place flower blossoms in a bowl of water. On Palm Sunday morning, she washes her face in the water because legend states that it will make her beautiful.

*T*he Sunday before Easter is called *Palm Sunday*, and it marks the beginning of Holy Week or the time of the passion of our Lord. On Palm Sunday, many churches pass out palm branches or tiny crosses made from palms in remembrance of Christ's triumphal entry into Jerusalem. When people shouted for joy and waved palm branches before Him as a gesture of respect and honor.

*O*n *Palm Sunday* in the Black Forest in Germany, tall poles are decorated with pussy willows, cross drawings, foliage, and streamers. They are carried to the church for a blessing and then placed in the dooryards of homes. In many parts of Germany, a wooden image of a donkey—the animal that carried Jesus into Jerusalem for His triumphal entry—is carried into the church. The people then go forward to touch it and to receive a blessing.

*I*n England, *Palm Sunday* was sometimes called Spanish Sunday, because children made a sweet drink from small pieces of Spanish licorice stirred into a bottle of water. The water used in this concoction had to come from a holy well, and a special pilgrimage was made to gather the water. The children circled the well three times, filled and shook their bottles, then merrily sipped their drinks.

"Easter Week"

Maundy Thursday

The Thursday before Easter is called *Maundy Thursday.* *Maundy* comes from a Latin word that means "a command," and it refers to when Jesus commanded His followers to love one another. On this special day many people, including world leaders, try to follow that command by giving maunds, or gifts, to the poor.

From a very early time in Church history, it was tradition for priests and others to wash the feet of twelve or more poor people on *Maundy Thursday* in remembrance of Christ washing His apostles' feet on the night before His crucifixion. In later years, gifts of money, food, and clothes were presented in addition to the ceremonial foot washing.

On *Holy Thursday* in Czechoslovakia the people eat "Judases" for breakfast. These little cakes are made from twisted dough. They look like rope, representing the fate of Judas Iscariot who hanged himself in grief after he turned Jesus over to His enemies. The cakes are served with honey.

"Easter Week"

Good Friday

On *Good Friday* morning, Bermudians enjoy hot cross buns. Their Easter breakfast is called the "Codfish and Banana Breakfast." Boneless, skinless salt cod is boiled along with peeled whole potatoes. The dish is then served with either olive oil poured over the top or a scoop of mayonnaise. A portion of sliced bananas accompanies the fish.

On *Good Friday* in Bermuda it is customary for children of all ages to fly kites. Various prizes are awarded to the children with the biggest, most beautiful, or longest-flown kites. This tradition can be traced back to a Bermudian Sunday School teacher who tried to explain Christ's ascension to Heaven to his class.

*F*or Christians, *Good Friday* is the most solemn day of the year. On this day, the passion and death of the Lord is remembered by church services of sorrow and thankfulness. In some parts of Europe this day is called Holy or Great Friday.

The French refer to Easter as Pâques, which begins with a solemn commemoration on *Good Friday.* As a sign of their mourning for Jesus, the French do not ring their church bells from Good Friday to Easter Sunday.

*F*or centuries it has been customary in England to play marbles on *Good Friday.* Some believe that it is linked to dice throwing that was practiced by Roman soldiers at the foot of the Cross. Every year on Good Friday in Sussex, England, a marble championship is held; and the champions are awarded a silver cup.

*O*n *Good Friday* at Ayot St. Peter in Hertfordshire, England, they ring the Nine Tailors for Our Lord's death. Ringing the Nine Tailors (or tellers) is an old custom that is used to inform the townspeople when someone has died. The bell rings nine times if a man has died, six times for a woman, and three times for a child. Then, after a brief pause, the bell rings again to indicate the age of the dead person. So, on Good Friday at Ayot St. Peter, the bell rings nine times for Christ; then the bell rings another thirty-three times to mark His age.

There is an inn in London called the Widow's Son, where each year on *Good Friday* a hot cross bun is placed in a basket next to many others from previous years. This tradition started in the early nineteenth century when the owner of the inn set aside a bun on each Good Friday in hopes that her sailor son, who was at sea, would safely return.

"Easter Week"

Easter Eve

*I*n the Wichita Mountains of Oklahoma, a six-hour Passion play takes place at Holy City. It is called the "Oklahoma Oberammergau," and it begins at midnight on *Easter Eve* and continues until sunrise. Approximately one hundred thousand people attend this play each year.

*I*n years past on *Easter Eve* in certain parts of Germany, giant oak wheels with straw-packed spokes were placed on the top of a hill and set on fire. These wheels were sometimes up to seven feet in diameter and often weighed over 800 pounds. People watched as they rolled down the hill, and the field where the wheel came to rest was considered blessed for a rich harvest.

*O*n *Easter Eve* in Lithuania, the people take two baskets to the church to be blessed. One basket contains small pieces of the food to be eaten for breakfast on Easter Sunday. The other basket holds bread and meat for the poor people who are waiting outside the church.

*I*n some Irish villages, a cake dance took place on *Easter Eve.* The man declared the best dancer was awarded a large cake, which he shared with his dance partner as well as the rest of the guests. The expression "He takes the cake" was derived from this custom.

In Greece, the Resurrection service is often held at midnight on *Easter Eve*. The people carry white candles decorated with ribbons and flowers. The lights are out in the church when the service begins. The priest enters carrying a lighted candle, and he says, "Come ye, partake of the never-setting Light and glorify Christ, who is risen from the dead." The people light their candles from his candle; then they pass their light on to the person beside them until the entire church is filled with light.

*O*n *Easter Eve,* many countries light fires to symbolize Christ as the Light of the World. This ceremony sometimes takes place outside of the church, while other times the fire is lighted in a metal container on the altar of the church.

The Paschal Candle is a large candle displayed near the altar of Roman Catholic churches, as well as some other churches, on *Easter Eve*. It remains there for forty days, and then it is taken down on Ascension Day, symbolizing that the Light of the World left on this day to ascend into Heaven.

"Easter Week"

Easter Sunday

From the time of the apostles, the early Christians observed a strict two-day fast from Good Friday until *Easter Sunday*, during which they did not eat or drink anything. Over time, a longer fasting period was introduced in preparation for Easter Sunday. During the third and fourth centuries, most churches gradually accepted the forty-day fasting period known as Lent. It begins on Ash Wednesday and ends on the Saturday before Easter Sunday.

*M*any scholars believe Christ's crucifixion occurred on Friday, April 17, in A.D. 30. If so, then Christ's resurrection took place on Sunday, April 19. For many years, however, people's opinions differed as to the actual date of the events, so in A.D. 325, at the Council of Nicaea, a group of Christian leaders decided that Easter should always be celebrated on the Sunday following the first full moon— that is on or after the vernal equinox. Hence, the date of *Easter Sunday* varies from year to year. It may come as early as March 22 or as late as April 25.

*I*t is believed that in 1609, the first sunrise service on *Easter Sunday* was held by a group of Spaniards exploring North America.

*C*adillac Mountain in Maine is the location of the first *Easter Sunday* sunrise service in the United States because it is the easternmost pinnacle of the country. The last ceremony on the mainland of the United States takes place in Yosemite National Park.

A legend popular in Great Britain and Ireland said that the sun always danced when it was rising on *Easter Sunday* morning because it was so excited that Christ had risen from His tomb. People believed that they could see it dancing if they climbed up to the top of a hill, so they gathered on hilltops to watch the sun rise on Easter morning.

*I*n Russia, *Easter Sunday* morning was filled with the sound of thousands of church bells ringing, for anyone who desired could go to the church and ring the bells. In the afternoon it was customary to visit friends; in fact, it was considered rude if you failed to visit every single one of your friends. The visitors always received the same greeting: "How kind of you! Come in! *Christohs voskress,* (Christ is risen)!"

*O*n *Easter Sunday* morning in Russia, the Ukraine, and Poland, the father of each house cuts up an egg blessed by a priest. He then divides the pieces among all the family members and wishes them a joyful and holy Easter. Then the family sits down to enjoy the rest of their breakfast.

In Venezuela an annual migration of freshwater turtles occurs every year around Easter. The turtles travel hundreds of miles to lay their eggs in the sand. The Venezuelans make jewelry from the turtle shells and cakes from the turtle meat are served as delicacies at the *Easter Sunday* meal.

In Finland, the term for Easter comes from the verb *päästä*, which means to get free. On *Easter Sunday*, people "get free from" the Lenten fast. It also signifies the day Jesus was freed from His tomb. They make a special Easter dessert called mämmi made from rye-meal and malt. Other foods served at the *Easter* meal are eggs, milk, blood sausage, pies, lamb, cheese, and veal.

*O*n *Easter Sunday* in Greece, it is customary to eat a special bread called the Bread of Christ. The top crust is marked with the Greek cross, which represents the Crucifixion. The bread loaf is also decorated with Easter eggs.

The meal on *Easter Sunday* in Poland is arguably the most elaborate of all the feasts served in all the countries that celebrate Easter. The Polish Easter table is decorated with greenery and the ornately designed *pysanki,* or Easter eggs. Either a lamb made of sugar or a lamb-shaped cake serves as the centerpiece of the table.

*I*n Portugal, Folar is a sweetbread served on *Easter Sunday.* It is baked in a flat, circular shape and decorated with hard-boiled eggs. The children give each other gifts of sugar-covered almonds that have been placed in small cornucopias made of colored paper.

149

In Russia, Poland, and other Eastern European countries, people greet each other on *Easter Sunday* by saying, "Christ is Risen!" The other person then responds, "He is risen indeed." They then usually exchange three kisses with each other. The Easter meal consists of the richest food the family can afford, and the priest blesses it before it is eaten.

*O*n *Easter Sunday* in Tampa, Florida, thirty-three white pigeons are released, symbolizing the number of years Christ lived on earth.

*I*n Europe, *Easter Sunday* is celebrated by lighting huge bonfires on hilltops and in church yards. The bonfires are commonly called "Judas fires" because effigies of Judas Iscariot, the betrayer of Jesus, are often burned in the fires.

*T*he *Paschal* or *Easter Chronicle,* a famous historical work written in A.D. 629 at Constantinople, recalls the events from the beginning of the creation of the world on until 629 A.D. The book is named the *Easter Chronicle* because Christ's resurrection on the first *Easter Sunday* was deemed to be the *most* important event in history.

*I*n some countries on *Easter Sunday*, families eat ham for their meal because the pig symbolizes wealth and prosperity. Another popular Easter dish is roast lamb. Lambs were often used in ancient sacrifices, and Jesus himself is often referred to as the Lamb of God—the ultimate Sacrifice for people's sins.

A Read-aloud Easter Story

Long ago in the land of Judea, an amazing man named Jesus walked through the countryside and went to the Temple for worship. Along with his disciples, Jesus preached about God's great love for all people. He told the people that he was God's Son—his *only* son. He said that he was the one sent by God—the Messiah, the Christ who would bring a sinful people back to God. He also healed the sick and performed many miracles. Soon crowds followed him everywhere he went.

The religious leaders in Jerusalem quickly became concerned as they heard of Jesus' growing popularity. One day, Jesus rode into Jerusalem on a donkey as crowds called him the King of Kings and threw palm branches in his path.

On that very day, the religious leaders decided Jesus had to be stopped at all cost. Later that week, he was arrested. Liars said bad things about him and said He had to die. The next day, Jesus was crucified between two thieves. His enemies rejoiced. They felt they had silenced His voice forever.

Jesus' disciples and close friends were very sad. They could not believe that their great leader was dead. Carefully, they took his body down from the cross, wrapped it in grave cloth, and placed it in a tomb. Then they stood watching with tear-stained faces as Roman soldiers sealed the tomb with an enormous boulder and placed guards nearby.

That might have been the end of this story—a good and gentle man, lied about and sent to his death. But it was not! Three days after Jesus was crucified, a few of his followers went to the tomb and found the big rock rolled away. The body of Jesus was gone! They saw the grave cloth that had encircled his body lying undisturbed and angels said Jesus had risen from the grave! Now it was Jesus' followers who rejoiced!

Throughout history, there have been many good and gentle men who have died for the message they preached. But, unlike Jesus, the stones that were placed over their graves continue to lock them in death. Only Jesus has Risen! Only Jesus is the mighty, only begotten Son of God!

Acknowledgments

Mary A. Lathbury (8), Venantius Fortunatus (12), Clarence W. Hull (14), Phillips Brooks (19,28), Martin Luther (34, 48), Donald Harvey Tippet (36), *Denham Tracts* (38), Desmond Tutu (40), Charles Wesley (43), Henry Ward (44), Lewiston Idaho *Tribune* (49), Thomas Kelley (52), Robert Browning (56), James Russell Lowell (60), Henry Hart Milman (101), Joyce Kilmet (92), John Keble (86), Christina Rossetti (87), Thomas Carlyle (88), James Ryder Randall (87), Thomas Kelly (92), Lyman Abbott (96), Thomas Blackburn (97), Clement of Alexandria (100), John Mason Neale (104), Frederick Beck (108), Thomas Scott (109).

Additional copies of this book and other titles from
Honor Books are available at your local bookstore
Look for the following titles throughout the seasons:

Happy Valentines Day
Happy Mother's Day
Happy Father's Day
Merry Christmas

If you have enjoyed this book or it has impacted your life,
we would like to hear from you.
Please contact us at:

Honor Books
Department E
P.O. Box 55388
Tulsa, Oklahoma 74155
Or by e-mail at *info@honorbooks.com*